YOUR KNOWLEDGE HAS VALUE

Lora Cvetanova

Review of Belinda Robnett's "How Long? How long? African-American women in the Struggle of Civil Rights"

GRIN Verlag

Bibliografische Information der Deutschen Nationalbibliothek:

Die Deutsche Bibliothek verzeichnet diese Publikation in der Deutschen National-
bibliografie; detaillierte bibliografische Daten sind im Internet über http://dnb.d-
nb.de/ abrufbar.

Imprint:

Copyright © 2014 GRIN Verlag GmbH
Druck und Bindung: Books on Demand GmbH, Norderstedt Germany
ISBN: 978-3-656-72262-5

This book at GRIN:

http://www.grin.com/en/e-book/278719/review-of-belinda-robnett-s-how-long-
how-long-african-american-women

GRIN - Your knowledge has value

Der GRIN Verlag publiziert seit 1998 wissenschaftliche Arbeiten von Studenten, Hochschullehrern und anderen Akademikern als eBook und gedrucktes Buch. Die Verlagswebsite www.grin.com ist die ideale Plattform zur Veröffentlichung von Hausarbeiten, Abschlussarbeiten, wissenschaftlichen Aufsätzen, Dissertationen und Fachbüchern.

Visit us on the internet:

http://www.grin.com/

http://www.facebook.com/grincom

http://www.twitter.com/grin_com

Université de Toulouse- Le Mirail

Département des Etudes Anglophone

Lora Cvetanova: Méthodologie d'anglais-Civilisation /Master 2

Review of

Belinda Robnett's How Long? How long? African-American

women in the Struggle of Civil Rights

2013/2014

Contents

Introduction

The African American Civil Rights Movement was a series of protests in the United States South from approximately 1955 through 1968. The overall goal of the Civil Rights Movement was to achieve racial equality before the law. Protest tactics were, overall, acts of civil disobedience. Rarely were they ever intended to be violent. From sit-ins to boycotts to marches, the activists involved in the Civil Rights Movement were vigilant and dedicated to the cause without being aggressive. While African-American men seemed to be the leaders in this epic movement, African-American women played a huge role behind the scenes and in the protests.

When discussing the American Civil Rights Movement, the names that seem to come up are those of prominent black men. While these men did enormous amounts of good during this movement, there are many women who seem to be poorly represented or credited. The number of writings about women in the struggle for civil rights movement continues to grow; new studies about the participation of black women appear. Through a comparative and analytical approach to the varieties of women's activism and the ways in which race, class, gender, and culture influence the Civil Rights movement, sociologist Belinda Robnett successfully attempts to provide an account of the participation of African American women in the movement.

In the fallowing paper I will first provide a historical background of the Civil Rights movement. Due to the fact that the book under study is a study of African- American women in the struggle for Civil Rights I will also provide a brief review of feminism and black feminism. From here on I will make a review of the book with a special attention to chapter

Two and the Montgomery Bus Boycott. Finally I will discuss Belinda Robnett's sources and the approaches and methods she uses to write her book.

Historical Background of the Civil Rights Movement

The Civil Rights movement is the title given to the effort to gain greater social, political and economic equality for black Americans which, it has been argued, emerged in its most recognisable form during the 1950s. To many, the Civil Rights movement was one of the greatest reform impulses of the twentieth century and its many victories have included such things as the Supreme Court decision in 1954 which declared segregation in public schools to be unconstitutional, the Montgomery bus boycott of 1955-1956, the passage of the Civil Rights Act of 1964 and the Voting rights act of 1965 (White, 1991, p.9)[2].In order to fully understand the Civil Rights Movement, one needs to go back to its origin. Most people believe that Rosa Parks[3] began the whole civil rights movement. As Robnett writes in her work, Mrs. Parks 'had been an active member of the NAACP for fifteen years at the time, she refused to relinquish her seat to a White men and had been thrown off the bus and arrested(1955).'(Robnett, page 57)

Further Robnett explains that 'This single act was to set in motion the heightened period of civil rights movement' (Robnett, page 58). According to the above quote we understand that she did in fact propel the Civil Rights movement to unprecedented heights but, we should not forget that its origin began in 1954 with Brown vs. Board of Education of Topeka[4].

---

[2] White, J. (1991) Martin Luther King, Jr., and the Civil Rights
Movement in America (British Association for American Studies)
[3] **Rosa Louise McCauley Parks** (February 4, 1913 – October 24, 2005) was an African-American civil rights activist, whom the United States Congress called "the first lady of civil rights" and "the mother of the freedom movement'
[4] **Brown v. Board of Education**, 347 U.S. 483 (1954), was a landmark United States Supreme Court case in which the Court declared state laws establishing separate public schools for black and white students unconstitutional.

Brown vs. Board of Education of Topeka was the cornerstone for change in American History as a whole. Before that, there was Plessy vs. Ferguson in 1896 that argued by declaring that state laws establish separate public schools for black and white students denied black children equal educational opportunity (Separate but equal doctrine)

There were also other events and case to provoke the movement such as the horrible death of Emmett Till in 1955, in which the main suspects were acquitted of beating, shooting, and throwing the fourteen year old African American boy in the Tallahatchie River, for "whistling at a white woman"[5]. In order to move into the future, one must let go of the past, and many people were not eager to abandon the beliefs that had been engrained in them since birth. Racial discrimination was present nationwide but the outrageous violence of African Americans in southern states became known as Jim Crow Laws[6]. Jim Crow Laws made it impossible for African Americans to be equals. It prohibited Blacks from marrying Caucasians, owning restaurants that served people of other races, drinking out of the same water fountain as whites, virtually separating races on every imaginable plane. According to these laws one understands that they are one of the causes for the deterioration of Society making once race feel inferior to another.

To conclude I may say that the whole purpose of the Civil Rights movement was to abandon this way of thinking and take a journey into the unknown, which was unity. Although historically Jim Crow Laws were abolished in the 1970's for good, the ideas, events, and feelings that emerged from this unfair practice of this law still haunted the south many years after.

---

[5] http://www.emmetttillmurder.com/ time and hour of the visit 04:01:2014, 15H59min.
[6] http://www.nps.gov/malu/forteachers/jim_crow_laws.htm, time and date of the visit 04:01: 2014, 16h 30 min

Feminism and Black Feminism

Having outlined briefly some if the main events causing the start of the movement, I will move on to the question of feminism in general and more precisely on black feminism.

Throughout most of our history women traditionally have had fewer rights than men. The early colonist operated under English common law which restricted rights while giving women additional duties in the house hold. The common law was predominately used regardless of once own religious preference. With the westward expansion through the Revolution of America came the changing roles of women in the household and workplace throughout early America. Women's roles during the colonial time of the 1700's were extremely challenging. Women in the household were expected to make clothing for use and retail, doctor and care for their family, clean and tend to livestock. During the early eighteenth century women were dominated by men from brothers and father's to their husband after marriage. During the nineteenth century, the women's rights movement was vastly significant because it led to suffrage and increased opportunities for women in the workforce.

Betty Friedan[7] writes that 'the only way for a woman, as for a man, to find herself, to know herself as a person, is by creative work of her own.'[8] The message here is that women need more than just a husband, children, and a home to feel fulfilled; women need independence and creative outlets, unrestrained by the pressures of society. Throughout much of history, women have struggled with the limited roles society imposed on them. The belief that women were intellectually inferior, physically weaker, and overemotional has reinforced

---

[7] **Betty Friedan** (February 4, 1921 – February 4, 2006) was an American writer, activist, and feminist. A leading figure in the women's movement in the United States,

[8] Betty Friedan, *The Feminine Mystique*. New York (New York, 1963) 62

stereotypes throughout history. In the 1960s, however, women challenged their roles as 'the happy little homemakers.'[9] Their story is the story of the Women's Liberation Movement.

But what about black women, who fights for their rights?!

E. Frances White[10] explains in her book that 'Black feminism emerged at the junction between antiracist and antisexists struggles. In this space, black women turned –and they continued to turn- their marginalization in both arenas into a vital political force'[11]. From the above citation we might guess that the Black Feminist Movement grew out of, and in response to, the Black Liberation Movement and the Women's Movement. What is more, Gloria Hul[12] states in her first chapter volum 9 that:

> In an effort to meet the needs of black women who felt they were being racially oppressed in the Women's Movement and sexually oppressed in the Black Liberation Movement, the Black Feminist Movement was formed. Black women who participated in the Black Liberation Movement and the Women's Movement were often discriminated against sexually and racially. Although neither all the black men nor all the white women in their respective movements were sexist and racist, enough of those with powerful influence were able to make the lives of the black women in these groups almost unbearable.'(Hull, vol9,chapter 1)[13].

---

[9] William L.O'neill. *Feminism in America : History*. (New Brunkswick and Oxford: Transaction Publishers, 1969) 308
[10] **E. Frances White** (born 1949) is a historian, author and academic.
[11] E. Frances, White; *Dark Continent of our bodies: Black Feminism and the Politics of Respectability*,(Philadelphia: Temple University Press, 2001) 25
[12] **Akasha Gloria Hull** (born December 6, 1944) is a poet, educator, writer, and critic whose work in African-American literature and as a Black feminist activist has helped shape Women's Studies.
[13] Gloria, Hull, T., eds. *But Some of Us Are Brave: Black Women's Studies* . Old Westburly, NY: Feminist Press, 1982, vol 9,chapter 1

Furthermore, Francis White reminds her readers that 'historians have generally ignored black women in slavery' and that 'an early attempt to redress this imbalance was Angela Davis's[14] influential work, *Reflections on the Black Women's role in the Community of Slaves*

(1971).'(White, ch 1, page 53).

Review of 'How long? How long?

Belinda Robnett is a modern sociologist and women's sutudy scholar who provides her readers with an interesting and exclusive account of the role of women in the Civil Rights movement. She challenges claims regarding sexism in the movement as she examines the complex web of relationships among the movement's leaders and rank-and-file. Robnett provides us with a 'socio-historical' analysis of the movement framed by a womanist/black feminist point of view. She also pays special attention to the leadership and the political roles women have in the movement. Belinda Robnett's *How Long? How Long?* gathers various , comprehensive accounts of African-American women activists from 1954-1965. To do so, she places black women at the center of her analysis within the broader history of the Southern Civil Rights movement. She also describes the complexity of women's experiences through the movement. Robnett examines the roles of activists within seven movement organizations National Association for the Advancement of Colored People (NAACP), the Women's Political Council (WPC), the Congress of Racial Equality (CORE), the Montgomery Improvement Association (MM the Southern Christian Leadership Conference (SCLC), the Student Nonviolent Coordinating Committee (SNCC), and the Mississippi Freedom Democratic Party (MFDP).

---

[14] **Angela Yvonne Davis** (born January 26, 1944) is an American political activist, scholar, Communist and author. She emerged as a nationally prominent counterculture activist and radical in the 1960s, as a leader of the Communist Party USA, and had close relations with the Black Panther Party through her involvement in the Civil Rights Movement despite never being an official member of the party.

For this study I will play special attention to chapter two- *Exclusion, Empowerment, and Partnership* where thanks to many oral testimonies from the women themselves, Robnett explores further the relationships among movement participants and thus, offers a critique of black leadership. Here, she examines the role of women in sustaining the 1955 Montgomery Bus Boycott. She correctly attributes the overall success of the 381-day boycott to the infrastructure provided by middle-class women of the Women's Political Council (WPC). She reaches the conclusion that 'what is abundantly clear is that African American women activists did not feel oppressed by their gender. Rather, they experienced feelings of empowerment and were inspired to transcend social constrains imposed by racists institutions and cultural forms (Robnett, chapter 2, page 51).' One of her main arguments is that 'women's status was gained through acts of courage, gender divisions, while quite real, were irrelevant to their day to day struggle to survive as a people'(Robnett, ch2, page 40). Through many quotations of testimonies of women who were actually involved in the movement as leaders (ex. Faye Bellamy[15], Septema Clark[16], Dorothy Cotton[17]) Robnett affirms that 'Women deferred to men was not at issue; the goal was the freedom of Black people and this could be achieved only through a cooperative effort' (Robnett, ch 2, p.43).

The above quote implies that the importance, here is not gender, but freedom. It shows that black people are united and fight for their rights together without posing the question of gender difference. However not once in her work Belinda Robnett talks about the supportive position women had in relation to men in the Montgomery bus boycott. She remind us that 'Though men became the formal leaders of the Montgomery Bus Boycott, it is clear that

---

[15] **Fay D. Bellamy Powell** (May 1, 1938 – January 5, 2013) was an African-American civil rights activist.
[16] **Septima Poinsette Clark** (May 3, 1898–December 15, 1987) was an American educator and civil rights activist. Clark developed the literacy and citizenship workshops that played an important role in the drive for voting rights and civil rights for African Americans in the American Civil Rights Movement.
[17] **Dorothy Cotton** (born 1930) was a leader of the 1960s African-American Civil Rights Movement and a member of the inner-circle of one of its main organizations, the Southern Christian Leadership Conference (SCLC).

without the support of the women bridge leaders and the community, their efforts would have proved fruitless.'(Robnett, p. 65). Moreover, thanks to Johnnie Carr's[18] memories, Robnett insists on the fact that women 'took responsibility for the well-being of those who were punished for boycott actions' (p. 66) and 'took responsibility for proving lunches'(p.66). Further in Mrs. Thelma Glass's[19] testimony one notices the repletion of the words ' service and support', 'give what type of services they could give to keep the movement going', 'people have to be fed', 'administrative support'.

It is evident that women were actually participating in the same way they would participate if they were at homes with their husbands. Cooking, caring for the well-being of others, help in administration, typing and writing letters are some of main duties of housewives. However, women's support is essential and thanks to it the Montgomery Bus Boycott was successful. Those interviews, with a key movement participants illuminate how, in the absence of access to formal leadership, women succeed to re-direct their energies in support of men while seeking opportunities for political self-expression and recognition. Here again, the collaboration of female and male leaders is evidenced as well as the conflicts and tensions women experienced in dealing with men, whose conventional views on women were gender-biased.

Another interesting Robnett's statement is that 'Given that women were most affected by the conditions on the busses, it is they who were most receptive to the initial suggestion of a bus boycott. Their acute feelings of humiliation, degradation, and anger propelled them to support the boycott despite the risk of arrest.'(Robnett, p.61). It is well known fact that women often relies on their emotions and feelings. Many of us have been accused by their

---

[18] **Johnnie Rebecca Daniels Carr** (January 26, 1911 – February 22, 2008) was a leader in the Civil Rights movement in the United States from 1955 until her death.
[19] **Thelma Glass** (May 16, 1916 – July 24, 2012) was an American civil rights activist, noted for helping to organize the Montgomery Bus Boycott of 1955, and a professor of geography

male fellows with words 'stop being silly and emotional' but in the context of African American struggle for freedom, women's emotions turn out to be essential for the movement and triggers the Montgomery boycott.

In the beginning of chapter one of her study Robnett challenges conventional theories of leadership as well as theories of social movement formation. She argues that 'a substantial proportion of the processes of recruitment, mobilization and sustenance of the Civil Rights Movement was performed by African- American women. Black women had limited access to key positions of formal leadership, even though they were well-represented among the rank and file.' (Robnett, p.17) Where 'bridge leaders,' is a term used by Robnett to refer to women who sewed in an important intermediate capacity; they were the vital link between nationally recognized male leaders and the masses of people.

Robnett's significant contribution to scholarship on African-American women's activism has deepened our understanding of the Civil Rights Movement and raised a number of critical questions worth further pursuit.

Belinda Robnett's sources and inspirations

I. Sources

To situate the book under study *How long? How long? African –American Women in the Struggle for Civil Rights,* so as we can understand better its place and significance in the field of sociology and women's study, I will provide a small list of other books on the same subject written in the 90s.

- *We Paid Our Dues: Women Trade Union Leaders of the Caribbean (1996), by A. Lynn Bolles; Gender and Jim Crow: Women and the Politics of White Supremacy in North Carolina(1896-1920)*, by Glenda Elizabeth Gilmore.

- *What a Woman Ought To Be and To Do: Black Professional Women Workers during the Jim Crow Era (1996),* by Stephanie J.

- *Invisible Southern Black Women Leaders in the Civil Rights Movement: The Triple Constraints of Gender, Race and Class(1993)* by McNair Barnett;

- *Triple Jeopardy': Black Women and the Growth of Feminist Consciousness in SNCC, (1964-1975)." In Still Lifting, Still Climbing: Contemporary African American Women's Activism, (1999)* by Anderson-Bricker, Kristin;

- *The Interstitial Politics of Black Feminist Organizations. Meridians: Feminism, Race, Transnationalism (2001) by Kimberly Springer, Women in the Civil Rights Movement: Trailblazers & Torchbearers 1941-1965(1993)*by Vicki L. Crawford;

- *Men Led: but Women Organized: Movement Participation of Women in the Mississippi Delta." In Women in the Civil Rights Movement: Trailblazers & Torchbearers, 1941-1965,* edited by Vicki L. Crawford, Jacqueline Anne Rouse, and Barbara Woods (1990);

All of the above authors place women in the center of their analyses. Some of these books provide detailed examinations of the political struggles of African-American and Afro-Caribbean women beginning in the 1800s and continuing into the next century. Each of them gives voice to black women, providing readers with new insights into the complexities of their daily struggles to survive. The authors show to their readers black women's strength and courage and in doing so give a new definition of the term political activism. *How long? How long? African –American Women in the Struggle for Civil Rights* has its special place among the many writings concerning African American women in the struggle.

Thanks to the comparative and analytical approach the author uses to prove her points, her book successfully rewrites history. The author uses testimonies to compare different women's views of the movement. For her study she uses a great number of sources such as: women's testimonies in phone interviews (25 interviewees), life histories, archives, scholarly accounts and other academically writings of the Civil Rights Movement period. While interviewing women she uses the method of asking one and the same question all the women in relation to their participation in the organization of the movement. Robnett divides the interviews in two categories: interviews of women in the movement and interviews obtained from the Civil Rights Documentation Project, Moorland Spingarn Research Centre at Howard University(5 interviews- Ella Baker, E.D.Nixon, Fannie Lou Hamer, Mary Lane, Rosa Parks), the Oral History Project at the Martin Luther King Jr. Centre for Non-Violent Social Change in Atlanta(4 interviews- Johnnie Carr, E.D. Nixon, Septima Clark, Virginia Durr), and from secondary sources(quotes and information from 18 women),(Robnett, appendix A, page 211).

For bigger certainty of her claims the author pays special attention to archival date which was double checked along her study. Some of the papers she uses for her research are: The Martin Luther King Jr. Papers, C. B. King Papers, Mississippi Freedom Democratic Party Papers,Oral History Series etc. Her secondary sources are writings that appeared in the second half of the 90s (from 1941 to 1999) some of which I cited in my list of books in the beginning of the chapter.

II. Inspirations

In the introduction of her work Belinda Robnett talks about her inspiration to write her book. We understand that she was a child in the time of the Civil Rights Movement. Because her family often experienced the inconvenience to be black in America one may say that her inspiration to write the book is genuine. Her history teachers, Mr. Watkins and Mr. Grubbs e encouraged her to study Black History. Her main inspiration is the need to know more about Black heroines of the movement.

> I thought of my grandmothers, mothers, and aunts who struggled alongside my grandfather, father, and uncles. This book is inspired by the struggles of these women and the realization that they (and I) needed to know more about our Black heroines. I wanted to know more about their work and struggle within the movement, and this I thought could only serve to strengthen us and our community. (Robnett, page 4)

Robnett also studies the work of women's rights activists such as Harriet Tubman, Sejourner Truth, Frances E. W. Harper, Ida B. Wells and Marry Church Terrell. She is deeply interested in the work of today's scholars: Margaret Somers and Gloriana Gibson. What is more, Robnett admits to have been criticizing other 'accounts of the movement as leaving women out, for reductively using the term activist to mean male' Robnett, page 5)

Conclusion

To sum up I would say that Belinda Robnett's book *How Long? How Long?* is interesting and useful book for those who are interested in sociology and women's studies. Robnett's work is a significant contribution to scholarship on African-American women's activism, and it has deepened our understanding of the Civil Rights Movement. Whatever her inspirations were, Belinda Robnett devoted her work to Black women and can be proud of the success it has. Her book is complex and provides us with a new view of the movement. It is a product of a serious research which includes various primary and secondary sources, testimonies of women, archive papers and many others.

Bibliography

Primary Sources

Robnett, Belinda. *How long? Howlong? African-American Women in the Struggle for Civil Rights.* NY and Oxford:Oxford University Press, 1999

Secondary Sources (Books)

Crawford, Vicki L.,Jackline Anne Rouse ,and Barbara Woods, eds. *Women in the Civil Rights Movement: Trailblazers and Torch bearers, 1941-1965. 1990*

Friedan, Betty. *The Feminine Mystique.* New York: New York, 1963

Hull, Gloria and Seung-Kyung Kim, eds. *But Some of Us are Brave: Black Women's studies.*Old Wesburly, Ny:Feminist Press, 1982

Klarman, Michael. *From Jim Crow to Civil Rights: The Supreme Court and the Struggle for Racial Equality.* Oxford: Oxford University Press, 2003

Morris, Aldon. *The Origins of the Civil Rights Movement: black Communities Organizing for Change. 1984*

O'Neil,L. William. *Feminism in America: a History.* Oxford: Transaction Publishers, 1989

Pelicher, Jane and Imelda Whelehan. *50 Key Concepts in Gender Studies.* London:SAGE Publications, 2004

White, E. Frances. *Dark Continent of Our Bodies: Black Feminism and the Politics of Respectability.* Philadelphia: Temple University Press, 2001

Secondary Sources (Sites)

http://www.emmetttillmurder.com/ time and hour of the visit 04:01:2014, 15H59min.
http://www.nps.gov/malu/forteachers/jim_crow_laws.htm, time and date of the visit 04:01: 2014, 16h 30 min
Cover Photo taken from: http://www.bu.edu/afam/2012/04/17/film-screening-reflections-unheard-black-women-in-civil-rights-by-nev-nnaji/ 05/01/2014 at 20H 00

All additional information about some prominent figures in the Civil Rights Movement which I included in the references is taken from Wikipedia.